Escape of the Leopard

Books by John Moffitt

This Narrow World · The Living Seed · Adam's Choice

John Moffitt

Escape of the Leopard

Harcourt Brace Jovanovich, Inc., New York

Printed in the United States of America

Some of the poems in this volume originally appeared in *America,
The Antioch Review, Approach, The Barat Review, Beloit Poetry
Journal, Chelsea, Commonweal, Granta, Kenyon Review, New Catholic
World, Poetry Review, Prism I* and *II, Quixote, Saturday Review,
Sewanee Review, The Virginia Quarterly Review, Voices, Wormwood
Review.*

Library of Congress Cataloging in Publication Data

Moffitt, John.
    Escape of the leopard.

    Poems.
    I.   Title.
PS3563.03E8   811'.5'4   73–11415
ISBN 0–15–129050–4

First edition
BCDE

Contents

1

The Cantata

And over it all, the sky reaching
pure as soft, high trumpets
out of the safe music of the past:
over the veiled power of young Southern
blacks, massed for songs of protest
but now suddenly persuaded to disband;
over the horror and the glory of
spent, nameless bodies, strewn haphazard
in jungle grass or shallow water,
crying out with their tall American or
slight Vietnamese shapes the divine sonship
even in this crude desecration:
yes, over the multitudinous weaving voices,
over it all, the everlasting sky
clean as trumpets, sure and strong,
sounding wholeness and light of day:
over the streets of a city,
calm now after the uneasy dark,
where the indifferent anonymous thin youth
walks back to his room after snatching
the paralytic beggar's money from his box;
over the beggar's unvoiced, ludicrous despair:
over it all, the comfortable and the strange,
bright and vigorous as freedom,
the trumpets of morning, floated
above the counterpoint of unnumbered
voices, infinitely involved,
and the dark, hollow drums of earth:
higher, stronger, freer, purer,
over the weak mouth and the ready
knife, as over the brief glance of
trust between friend and honored friend,
the treasuring look the Puerto Rican
father bends on his half-naked son.

In February Sun

The red bud of the hawthorn,
The red skin
Of the twig, stiletto stab of spur
Along the polished stem,
Jointure of stem,
Red-green, upon the gray-green branch,
The twist and flow
Of snake-smooth skin to rugged bark,
The reach, the homeward
Plunge of crabbèd trunk to soil,
To unseen frost-held root
Within the watching thought.

The Signals

What signals are these that keep reaching us
Across the confused passage of our days—
Strong as the nearby voice of an announcer
Through the wall, whose bold inflections are
Clearly audible but whose fine distinctions
Muffled wholly; sharp as the harsh calls
Crow sentries signal with, in their uncracked
Code, to a scattered flock across a cornfield
From strategic watch-trees in first fall;
Strange as the undecipherable move
An Egyptian guard made, once, in the Cairo
Museum, when he took by the hand the only
Visitor in the Old Kingdom Room
And showed him eagerly some simple frescoes
Of water birds painted in green and blue?

Will, one day, the luminous inflections
Coalesce into sense, the outlandish symbols
Yield our puzzling more than a wild guess?
Like the sea sounds spoken by a conch shell
Pressed on the ear, perhaps they tell us really
Something from ourselves, and if we managed
The wit to master them, they would turn out
As simple as our guesses make them strange.

Among the Waves

Agile, on the alert,
The little grebe, gray-brown
Upon the luminous blown
Green of the reservoir—
Floating, cocky and half wild,
In seeming unconcern—
Dives now, and dives again
Straightway down,
Out of the naked February cold.

These vivid waves that swell
Under an immense blue cloudless sky,
This bird, so noticeable
Because it paddles here alone,
This diving out of sight
And staying hidden two whole
Minutes—do they speak
In broken hints to the mind
Something more actual, more real?

Floated down between
The varying waves of thought,
Cradled close among
The myriad crests of the bouncing waves—
This is no bold object,
Like sky or waterfowl,
That can be grasped or singled out.
It is not, when these are;
It is, when they are not.

Only when, momently,
Sight ceases, when the blown
Waves and the small bird's byplay
Vanish, that dazzling dark,
Nearer than breathing, near

As the coldness in cold air—
Speaking a vivid tongue
Beyond the dimnesses of sight—
Momently floats here.

The Change

He stood inside the storm
And from a safe window
Watched as snowflakes swirled
And swarmed about the walls.
He felt storm-winds strain
Above, behind, around,
And sensed a soundless sound
Of space and solitude
Waiting past the stars
To say itself aloud.

He saw the light seep out
And dangerous night descend
And heard the snow turn
Into dissolving rain,
And started to the quake
Of thunder in the air,
Which cavernously answered
Lightning's muffled light.
He felt the air go calm
And the winds abate.

And all that night he slept
To the continuous pound
Racing raindrops made
On the roof and panes.
And when he woke to dawn
The world outside was bare,
But in his own shut room
Instead of habit's voice
Spoke the soundless sound
Of solitude and space.

Direction

(Late Winter: High Noon)

Walk away from the sun
And the bare branches show
Distinct, every one
Matched with its own shadow,
And each exact bole
Rounds out as if designed
By a traditionalist
Master of a bygone
Epoch: nothing here
But has its precise place,
Each score of bark or narrow
Stem's obliquities
Caught fast in time, as though
With photographic flair
Time meant to keep them so,
Immediate and secure.

But walk against the sun
And everything seems new,
Twigs, branches, stems, begin
Converting, in plain view,
To webs of fine-spun light
Drawn on a shadow base
As in some abstract artist's
Scheme, where shape gives place
To substance: no tree but
Is haloed with thin fires,
Timeless and remote,
Whose every detail blurs,
And as exact resemblance
Takes a doubtful face,
Twigs and stems blossom
With unguessed potencies.

Of the Light

Everything in the light
Is of the light, as well:
This bent cherry branch
Close budded for new bloom,
Threading emptiness
With a sure, native skill,
Was drawn out by the poured
Light of returning suns;
Not one visible plant
In these awakened fields
But shapes its structure by
Or feeds its substance from
That earliest element;
And not plants alone,
For the fine stuff of which
Those flesh-built vehicles
Of worms or vertebrates
That soon will forage here
About this cherry tree
Are made, this too remains
As by-product of some
Ancient holocaust
That shed, before it failed,
A glow through space and time.
Even the inciting cause
Of quivering protoplasm,
Which gathered unobserved
Out of rich sea slime;
The preordaining source
Of each primordial cell's
Eventual aptitude
To feel, taste, smell, or hear—
What cause else was it
But the same agency
That implemented sight?

God said, "Let there be light,"
And there was, and of that
First fertilizing charge
Issued all things, and all
Their inbred consequence.
All atoms, all live cells
Of rocks, trees, animals,
And all gross shapes, besides,
In their beginnings and
Their primes and their decays,
Are wedded in this source,
Woven of its life,
Webbed of its warp and woof;
All motions and all moods
Of creatures, as of tides,
Each turn of art or science
In men's inheritance,
Or meditation on
The cosmic interplay
Of chance and fixed design,
Budded from this stem.
And so it is that all
Living creatures bear
Allegiance to pure light
And to its presence yield
A deeply wrought response;
So, also, that I hymn
Light's first conceiving here
And all its many-hued
Turns and conjurings,
Along with these sun glints
Down this bent cherry branch
And their promise, too,
Of brief white blossoming
For sunlight to float through.

The Flowering Corpse

The working of this slow, warm haze
That haunts and hovers among these
Leafing elm and sycamore boughs—
Which breathe, in filtered morning sun,
Pale fawns and lavenders and dim
Greens—evokes, here at the stopped
End of the street, a spell of calm
For vague enchantments to pause on:
Such breath of magic, it would seem,
As owns prerogative and power
To blossom in sheer vacuum.

Yet what does such gold-pollen bloom
Among flame-budded, kindling trees
Elicit its enchantments from,
If not the very grime and blight
Of this cross-street's open end,
Leading blankly through the thin
Atmosphere of bare unease
That pauseless hungers daily pour
About men's repetitious ways—
And that a veil of leaf-sewn light
Gives respite from, this early hour?

Is there no blossoming that breathes
Out of some pure necessity,
Unmatched by a crude opposite?
Whose clear persuadings were not fed
On men's ungovernable urge
To gainsay what would counter it?
Frilled orchids feed on sickly air
And spend their rareness for the elect;
This flowering, squandered for the lost,
Feeds its magic on a corpse
That floated leafage veils from sight.

Breathing of Wind

The wind presses his snout
Against the panes
And breathes in the spring night
Till he almost bursts them in;
And as he goes about
His wayward businesses
You wonder whether he means
Evil or means good—
So small the difference is
Between the moving of
A demon and a god.

2

Staying Just There

Have you seen—have you not seen,
In sun-still spring or autumn air,
As you perhaps went idling down
Some leaf-shuttered country lane,
A single smallish fly, one that was
Neither fruit fly nor bluebottle
But of a size somewhere in between,

Hover in the mild air, balancing on
Frail, diaphanous, glistening wings—
Keeping in that one place as if
Its whole occupation was to stay
Just there; then suddenly rocketing
Forward, upward, and to the rear
In a vertiginous circular swing,

But coming always back and back
To the same point where it had been
Balancing earlier—not, again,
For any more noticeable reason than
The sheer pleasure of floating in
That stillness of space; or, if a less
Innocent logic would best explain
Such a performing, just for the sake
Of not looking elsewhere in that time
Its urges told it to meditate there:

As you yourself, bright fool, might well
Be doing, in your own singular way,
Were you the natural balancer that
Some others about you seem to be—
In their alternate soaring and hovering
Light and free as the fly's maneuvering.

Have you seen—have you not seen?

Hummingbird-Heart

Greedy bird, you are not more exasperating
Than a certain small person of my preference—
You who have formed the alarming habit
Of drinking only out of the Audubon Society's
Artfully camouflaged feeding-tube
Sugar and water mixed in precise proportions.
Shy, fascinating creature—
Shrilling to me impatiently to move away
Whenever I loom too near for your electric
Shape to dart down to flower level unafraid—
How was I to know you would prove
So fond of refined cane sugar as to make me
Fill your tube two and even three times a day?
How was I to know, amiable pest,
That you would take whatever I have to give—
Importunate, insatiable—
With never a thought of sharing your exquisite small
Self for more than the space contained
Between the opening and shutting of an eye?

The Lover and the Raccoon

Only when I had sat down to ponder
My great good luck, there on the high bare
Rock, under the pine, the ancient
Tall spare one, yellowed with dying
Sun: how I had been delivered
At last into love's hands and known its
Quietest healing—
                        half listening to
The late notes of a catbird faithfully
Singing its wholeness, and seated where
Dumbly I opened a torn wound days
Earlier and found no peace—
                        though now
Suddenly I owned what I had sought for—

Only then I saw your tail hanging
Ringed like a tiger's, saw your woolly
Haunches that showed frowzy behind,
Saw all your grayish shape draped over
The high dead limb, and how your questioning
Eyes followed each move of mine,
Crouched on the pine as if you thought you
Were invisible so, and wondered that there
Should be in you the least fear, asking
Aloud, how, anxious face, when I
Sat there so full of love—
                        I who had
Wrestled with a gray void inside my
Chest, days long, but knew now I was
Loved and taken—
                        how it was that all
This love was not enough to tell you
Now it was safe to maneuver to a less
Precarious perch: holding up empty
Hands to show you I meant no slightest
Harm,

        and looking in your sharp
Black-masked eyes still following each
Move of mine, vowed that as none else
Knew my luck, so none should hear
Of you—
            so warm and singing I was
Inside, so yellowed through with love's
Quietest glow;
                and only when I turned away,
Seeing you still obstinately perched
Uncomfortable up there with pine and sky,
Did you decide it was time to stir
Discreetly, scratching each pointed ear
With its appropriate hand, once I
Had moved some way off, as if to say
You meant to sit just where you were.

Wherever I Speed

In the wake of small vessels
In the white glittering
On the glass-dark wave
Always I am moving,

By the sparse lonely willows
By the low green bending
Through the foam parted
And whirled swiftly backward:

As I spin down the valleys
As I scale the storm-clouds
Wherever I speed
About this earth's body,

In the wake of small vessels
In the white glittering
On the glass-dark wave
Always I am moving.

The Field

Through the abandoned field
Hemmed with outcropping rock
Red raspberries grow wild
In early-morning sun:
Under gray-backed leaves
Along the spiny canes
Bright crimson berries hang.
Upon the rise beyond,
Down thin rock crevices
Trim huckleberries run,
Whose fleshy round fruits show
Sky-blue against the green;
While at the grasses' edge
Dewberries glisten, black
And red, on stringy vines
That reach along the rock;
And strangely out of place,
A growth of wintergreen,
Luxuriantly in bloom,
Crowds in a narrow seam.

All these gifts, I raise
In my accepting hands
This quiet morning time,
And of them make offering,
With each fresh sight or sound
Of insect, bird, or flower
That states its relevance,
To the hid god who marks
The myriad ways of sense
And goes with men always;
Sure that precisely here
Within this tenantless
Wild field, owned solely by
Things unabashedly free,

Spreads a sufficient world
—In its own reference
As full as any else
Of meanings and pursuits—
Ready to put to test
An hour's capacities.

The Two Minnows

Weed-green above, cloud-white below,
Two minnows darted in the pool.
The pool was long and flat and full
And the short fish sped to and fro.
He watched them shoot from side to side.
The pool was twice as long as wide.
He watched a quarter hour or so,
And as they zigzagged through the dark
Patches that marked hidden rock,
A quiet took him through and through.

And he himself became the pair
That tirelessly cavorted there,
Became the waters' muted glow,
The floor of mud that spread beneath
And the pale water weeds' thin growth,
Became the banks they fastened to,
The opaque clouds the minnows stirred
While pausing near the oozy mud,
When the webbed fins were turning slow.

Stretched out on damp turf he lay,
Heedless of place or time of day,
Divorced from all identity
That might have something else to do,
Till the fish zigzagged at full speed
To the pool's other end—and so
Became his scattered self again
And shakily got up to go.

This Chip of Spotted Stone

This chip of spotted stone
In my hand,
Found just by the skyward edge
Of that frost-cracked granite ridge:
White flecks on a black ground—
In it I own no less than
The measurable extent
Of the whole firmament.

Itself a galaxy in miniature,
Who knows how time-lost far
The clustered molecules
That build its tight-packed solidness
—And the scarce atoms, too,
That structure them—
Reach back, in this identical form,
Into the artery of time?

And yet, beyond those shapes
The atoms and the molecules
Have worn, these eons while they spun
Along with earth,
And before then, in the rolled clouds
Of stellar gas, which churned
Through longer eons still
Into a live star's mass—

Beyond those shapes, who knows
What stretches of galactic years
Reach back
The earliest beats of thought,
In what vast brain began
That aboriginal restlessness?
If you can say "begin"
Of something that

Dilates and contracts
To the slow systole and diastole
Of a cosmic heart—

Something that, even now,
Throbs in this flecked chip of stone,
Throbs in all things
—In stuff of cloud or galaxy
As in the flesh of man—
Ready to be caught and known
By any mind or microscope
Acute enough to trace
The tremor of its constant pulse.

Clear Evening

Across the beach of sky
Night's imperceptible flow
Filters its sure way—
Deceiving in that while
Its depth increases, still
Some glimmer from beneath
Keeps on shining through,
So that as long as you
Watch only in one place
No change seems to occur,
And, before you know,
The tide has filtered quite
Across that dry expanse
And reaches for the shell
Of new moon that lies there
Half hidden in blue sands,
When, having risen and flowed
Even to the burnt orange
Mainland of the west,
It wraps all else from view:
Only that shell persists,
Increasingly intense
Under night's flood tide,
And a few starfish glints
Scattered near about,
To hint the beach it hides.

The Well

After the darkness clears,
As you look down you see
Moving on the waters
Dim lights and figurings;
And up the mossy sides
Thin courses running round
Of squarely laid field stone
Grow plainer to your eye.

Let the bent bucket down
And pay the worn rope slow,
Hear the echoey splash
And draw the rope again.
Do not perplex yourself
To picture the blind stream
That flows on some rock shelf
Under this thirsty hill.

Why should you ask how low
The water table lies,
How cold the temperature,
How high the lime content?
It is enough to know
A watercourse flows here
Whose constant excess will
Serve you the summer through.

3

The Guardian

(After Henri Rousseau's "La Guerre")

Glee-eyed, there you go, seized in my mind, mad woman,
More than naked in your white, jagged-edge shift,
Absently riding the black fiend mare of the long
Neck and small intolerable head—your two hands
Brandishing the flashed sword and smoking torch,
Your hair disheveled as the brush of frenetic mane—
With her, the intent steed precariously beneath you, leaping
Over the limp pink-gray bodies of the innumerable dead.

There you go, guardian of all places of violence and blood,
Aloof, exulting, presence inevitable yet not to be believed,
Friend and familiar to the few crows that peck and pull
Always at the torn flesh and take no time to look after you,
Riding to nowhere, speeding forever in a steep silence
That never moves from where it is—endlessly passing
Those twists of blasted trees, which scar the glorious
Sunset rose and blue glow of an unheeding laughter

That mocks my helplessness and claims me for its own.

The Victims

The warm night of the thick, half-bare
Black, lying spread-eagled by the
Unfrequented road, his head lost in dusty
Weeds—the just slightly hairy backs of his
Thighs bursting toward you under the worn
Work shorts, the shallow-curved
Arc his buttocks make above the sharp
Inner wedge of his thighs, and beyond,
The curved furrow of the naked spine
Between paired rounds of ribs: all these
Speaking the rhythms of well-used love
And song and laughter unashamed—cries
Now the fact of a curdled, searing
Hate, now first articulate in the single
Bullet that spat from a passing car:
Cries, too, dark hints of blood demanded in
Return, yet for a whole people,
Promise of a believable reward at last.

And there, down the road, in the half-burnt
Chapel, looking out on you, the cool dawn of the
Sinewy Hebrew shape—arrow of flesh, hands pierced
Each by a single nail, streaming black blood,
The head drooped in final yielding, the face
Sweated, spat upon, stained beyond knowing,
The bare, hairless body, rag at the waist,
Drained wax of the ribs and loins: all these
Speaking only a lasting fund of love;
The spike in the twisted feet, a poor
Failure of cherished friends; the tired neck,
And the arms outstretched in willed acceptance,
A tenderness unguessed, and to this
End of time never yet hinting revenge, but
Always gentler expounding to a capable

Undistracted watcher their timeless key—
Offers and offers still to ears unhearing
The bright never quite believable reward.

The Holocaust

He sat inside the mangled plane
Where it lay helpless on the ground,
His safety belt still fastened on,
And all about him he could hear
Relaxing metal and hurt men:
"They said the tail's the safest place,"
He kept repeating in his mind.
Too stunned to shift from where he sat
By the obscene explosion's force,
Too tired to feel his injured side
Or mark the throbbing in his head,
He sat erect and looked straight on
Into the warm wind from in front,
As blood eased gently down his neck
Out of a partly severed vein.

Held in a languorous restraint,
He felt no urge to turn his glance
Toward what was sitting by his side,
But only stared ahead of him
At the acutely warped door frame.
The wind grew hotter in his face,
But though his mind had come alert,
Somehow he made no move to unloose
His belt and try to reach the door.
Erect he sat inside the plane,
Almost, he fancied, by firm choice,
And as the weakness grew on him
He felt his hands and feet grow numb,
Quiet and watching what would come
From the wrecked fuselage out front.

And with a searing hiss it came
Right down the middle of the aisle,
Fed on a tongue of gasoline

He saw but could no longer smell:
At first a narrow snake of light
With smoking feathers streaked behind,
And then a swelling dragon shape,
Which breathed a gust and then a glare
Of whirling, blind, engulfing heat
That swallowed the whole pent-up space
And crunched the glass and seized the paint
And climbed the curtains in one leap
And licked his hair and eyebrows off
And chewed the clothes across his chest
Till glowing strips unpeeled from him.

Then, as he sat within his trance,
He saw his skin sear, split, and curl
And for a moment felt an edge
Of anguish bite into his flesh
While the heat gnawed his fingernails;
Then watched his bared arm muscles swell
And fester to a vicious red;
Yet still the hurt was not enough
To dazzle out his watchfulness
Till the charred clothing dropped away
And left him naked to the waist,
When a clear pool of liquid pain
Boiled up briefly at his groin
As the flame racked his manhood's core,
Then mercifully melted sense.

Now, as he breathed the livid air,
He felt a seething in his brain;
Then all at once across his sight
A glaze of dancing bubbles spread,
Sealing awareness up inside;
And a great wave of freezing heat
Closed on him, and identity
Collected downward to his heart,

And all he was, was one sheer mass
Of blazing, unplumbed consciousness,
Which, suffering extreme of pain,
Yet suffered it with unbent will
As if his bearing it dissolved
All guilt, his own and every man's,
Earned in all history before.

And as the wrenching metal's flare
Blotted out space and time and breath,
Serene, though steeped in ecstasies
Of pain, he waited, still alert,
Till his full measure should pour out,
And in that instant issued forth
Into the universal fire.

Along the Curb

Deathward all are failing:
Deathward the thin boy,
Arms flailing,
Body ripped with joy,
Darting, screaming,
Lost in curbstone play;
Deathward the dog,
Dirty but not unloved,
Hotly biting the red
Ball as it rolls free;
Deathward the mother, calling
Out of the third-floor window,
Calling that supper's ready,
Calling to watch for the cars—
Deathward, deathward,
The quick forms failing.

But the lunge of the boy's
Delight, his flinging laughter,
And the dog's
Easy comradeliness,
The implied caress
In the anxious mother's call—
Surely these, being shown
Only in instant gleams,
Bear a witness
Out of the reach of change;
These—though they briefly move
Through time and casualty
As the quick forms go—
Deathward with the failing
Forms forever fail,
Deathward, but not to die.

The Day Before the End

(*October 24, 1962*)

On this last day
The world is beautiful with doom:
Appropriately
A blue perfection rides the air
And all the houses shine
Distinct, electrical,
As if yet to enforce the old deceit
We so long nursed, that life was meaningful.

The wide city wears
An aspect of high holy day,
The streets are silent and the citizens few,
Each object, far or near,
Stands clean and right,
And men's faces take on
Solemnity and a quiet calm,
While the mind gathers to its last insight,
Seeing for the first time the weight
Of judgment in the thought
That I am who I am
And things are what they are.

Let us not, then, grudge fate its say
On this last day.

Conditional

If I could unremember
The cadence of a voice,
The quiet of a manner,
The candor of a face,

I'd be as fit as ever
To walk the world at ease,
Smiling at one or other,
Sharing their urgencies.

But still the soleness looms
Of one too true to tell,
Whose pauseless quest disdains
Its mortal interval—

Of one who cannot measure
The ferment I endure,
Surmising, would surrender
All that incites desire.

And so, perplexed, I ponder
The peace that must await
If I could unremember
—Or you could unforget.

At the Last Hour

"Billy Budd! Billy Budd!" cried Starry Vere.
What else was there to cry at the last hour?
Haven't you known the pang, the insane reach
For purity beyond claim, spoiled in the touch,
The irrepressible trust that, say what you will,
Each man jack of us harbors in his soul
To be the ridgepole for his firmament,
Prop of his every move—till, all being spent,
Stop of the pulse and the breath undoes
This joke of living, and its brittle stress
Falters, the enticing lie goes under,
And long peace comes? No wonder, no wonder
With his last breath, everything else said,
Starry Vere cried, "Billy Budd! Billy Budd!"

Sacrament

Put up your arm, dearest,
Let me smell the sweat:
Here for one blind moment
Let us forget
The iron bit that clamps
Our churning, willful souls,
The blank signpost that says
Thus far, no farther pass
Toward the improbable goal
That spurs hoping on:
Here in this brief act
Of shared simplicity
Let us pretend
All journeyings begin,
All destinations lie.

The Bargain

In this hot controversy of our loves
To buy the person of the Anointed One,
I thought myself for certain quite shut out,
For all I held was one thin copper mite
And straightway, when the earliest bids began,
I rashly offered up my battered coin
As price for the chaste essence that he is,
While you, more shrewdly, laid a talent down
Of silver, playing for his still warm flesh.

The Auctioneer cried: "Going—going—gone!"
And bade his corporals bear the exhibit off
To those who claimed it. Then two fellows rose
And lifted his dark presence from the cross
Where all these hours it had endured display,
And dealt to each the part his monies won:
To you the part of passing and desire,
To me the unwed breath, whose modest loss
Seemed in your eyes immeasurably slight
Beside the tortured magic of his face.

And yet it seems to me that with my part
I have the better bargain, after all,
For what of him I own is the mock of time,
The flowering stem whence fresh beginnings come;
Yours but a twisted husk, already blown,
The proper fee of timely bargaining.
I have the better bargain, after all:
You have the body, but I have the soul.

4

Rebel Poet

No, I'll not polish,
That would be
Proof of a smallish
Bent of mind:

Let my way, rather,
Be to find
Quickness to gather,
Day by day,

Whatever gleanings
Sight can seize
Of the hid meanings
Nature takes

Out of its daily
Bag of tricks,
And with them rawly
Sound my praise

For the sly Maker
Of things here,
Who creates quicker
Even than thought

And whose outrageous
Oversights
Grow more contagious
Year by year.

Cock of the Walk

How is it that, once having seen
Clear through to the essential shallowness and
Indecision of the majority, the superior cock
Now flaps side-thumping wings and shouts exuberant
Defiance at the sun? His beady yellow eyes
Snapping, his auburn neck arched, and burnished
Tail-feathers astir, how is it that he yet
Fancies to bend the pert younger roosters and the
Soulless hens of all ages to his express and
Immediate will?

Is it sheer inconsistency, this
Taking of pride in the subservience of a
Flock he more than half scorns? Does it, on the
Other hand, betray a modulated adjusting to his
Natural concern, even fondness, for those
Among whom he was reared and somehow feels
Comfortable, even though fully aware of their
Ineptitude? Or would it simply prove a bold cock's
Felt need to impose himself intellectually and
Emotionally as well as through the more obvious
Channels?

Could it just be, again, that with
All the quick tilting of that red-combed head and
Sharp glancing of those angry eyes, he hasn't really
Seen clear through to the shallowness and the
Indecision of the majority he so confidently
Commands?

A Concert at Williams College by the Budapest String Quartet

Beethoven: String Quartet in F minor, Opus 95
Bartók: String Quartet No. 6
Schubert: String Quartet in A minor, Opus 29

Old Ludwig tossed his shaggy mane
And Mr. Chapin smiled and bowed,
Ralph Adams Cram, quite out of sorts,
Muttered dejectedly, off stage,
As the four fiddlers bravely ploughed
In simulated peace or rage
Through movements elegant or loud,
While All-America supplied
The motley, animated throng
Of crew-cut youths and beetle-browed
Professors, wives, and ancient ladies
With formal, unrelenting faces,
Who, packed inside the steaming oven
Properly known as Chapin Hall,
Could be relied on not to applaud
The Schubert, Bartók, and Beethoven
Except at the appointed places.

Ralph Adams Cram, as Ludwig thundered,
Scratched his poll and looked about
Through chinks in the dim organ loft
At the broad ornamental vault,
Which served for sounding board and ceiling,
Noted where paint was worn and peeling,
Sweated and fidgeted and wondered
In Gothic horror and amazement
Why he had let himself be drawn
Into this dubious engagement
When he could better pass the time
Gossiping with St. John the Divine,
And thought it wise not to recall
How he had dreamt up this quaint hall.

Though Mr. Chapin bowed and smiled,
Enraptured with the spreading scene
His past munificence made possible
(Cheering old Ludwig's humors on
In an approving undertone
And thinking Cram far too irascible),
He kept on whispering to himself
Between wild bursts of windy music,
It might have done a deal more good
If only somehow he had thought
To hold back half the total cost
Of this vast barn that bore his name,
To eke out his own livelihood.

But Ludwig, fuming to fling free
From music's throttling tyranny
And pour his thirsty soul a rest,
Growing more nervous every minute
As the two other boys took turns,
Swore up and down he'd not again
Concoct such bombast to be played
By any set of fiddling men,
For though the world's capriciousness
Still took his music for the best,
Considering people's altered ears
There wasn't any future in it.

What the four furious fiddlers thought,
On the wide, lonely, flood-lit stage,
Of the performance they turned out,
Or of the throng they played it at,
Or of the busy stuff they played,
No meddling eavesdropper could creep
Quite near enough to learn, precisely.
As for the crew-cuts', ancient ladies',
Professors', and attendant wives'
Views on the skitterings they heard,

Which cost their graces not a penny
And filled an evening rather nicely,
We'd hasten to retail them all,
But happily they hadn't any.

Mr. Chapin: A generous benefactor of Williams College, who presented it with the large hall now bearing his name, built, it is said, at huge cost. He was ruined in the financial crash of 1929, whereupon the college reciprocated by helping to support him till his death a few years later.

Ralph Adams Cram: The noted architect of the Cathedral of St. John the Divine in New York, distinguished in his later years for his interest in the early Gothic style. Chapin Hall, designed near the start of his career, is in an eclectic style and has a highly ornate barrel-vaulted ceiling.

Date: December 5, 1956

Frost on Frost

(*With Apologies to Himself*)

I like the man
And I like the thought
(A good lot of it),
And the way his snows
Shake down on us
When, without much fuss,
He slyly arranges
Apocryphal changes
Of homely wisdom
To build a conceit.
And as for the rest
Of his furbelows,
Like any good sport
I'm game to condone 'em
(*De mortuis,* as they say,
Nil nisi bonum)
Now that he's gone
And given us the slip,
And can't stab us back
With his leer or his lip
—Except for the lurch
Of his rhythm's beat,
The compulsive wham
When the line cuts short,
Of an old tin pan
In a bad boy's hand,
Or the heavy stomp,
When the line draws long,
Of a wooden leg
On a cobblestone street.

I like the man,
As you heard me say,
And I like the thought

(Where it's not too flat),
And I hail the lines
When the speech flows smooth
And limpid as all your
Best lines should;
And I'll even condone
That ponderous coy
New England wit,
And the innocent frills
That accompany it,
Which seem to imply
Self-satisfied joy—
But the rhythm's beat
When the line cuts short,
Or its dogged pound
When it undertakes
To spell out that crusty
Five-stress span,
That hippety-hop
Bang of the pan
Or stomp of the foot,
Which often, so often,
Makes you wonder
When, for God's sake,
When it will stop—
I can't condone that,
I can't condone that.

Nightmare's Nest

(A Horselaugh from Pegasus' Modern Mews)

Wither my blind bones
Fat slug of summer
(Summer that never
Comes, coming always
Or always passing over):
Sucking my sap
Slowly wrap me in shallow slime.

Wander-crazy wind
Wind in the hissing cones
Choke your moaning:
Shrunk to an eerie nearness
Blow me deaf asleep
Smoothly, coolly
Soothe the teasing itch in the wound.

Fat shrug of slumber
Womb of the murdering worm
Drugging my fear
Cover, close lover
My clogged cancerous waste:
Stiff wrap me
Smother me over and over and over.

Surmise

Heaven is out of hearing,
But God conceivably
Could find it rather wearing
To pass eternity

Listening to lean angels
Clad in organdie,
Nimbuses, and bangles
Echoing Emily.

The Itch Mite

Love's an itch mite lodged between the thighs,
Chafing some tender, private part,
Best plucked and crushed before it multiplies
Beyond the patience of the heart

To probe each crevice of its cloistered home,
Each hidden, shrinking, hair-stopped pore
Against the naughty animalculum—
Costing Blue Ointment for a cure.

Cockroach

Cockroach from the kitchen sink,
As you scuttle for the wall
Should you stir yourself to think,
Might it not appear to you
Something less than wonderful,
Something for a roach to rue,
That the quick-as-lightning dashes
Your resourcefulness unleashes
Get you nowhere, seconds late,
Leave you squashed and out-of-date,
Being matched uncannily
By your host's ability
To prefigure all your moves?

Might it not perplex your faith
To observe, from underneath,
With your final, feeble breath,
That the God whose love approves
Every creature, proud or mean,
Has endowed hands, feet, and brain
With divine agility?
Might you not incline to wonder
With a lively cockroach candor
How a love that implements
Equally both great and small
In a more than mocking sense
Can be called all-merciful?

5

Escape of the Leopard

The Leopard marches back and forth
Behind the stripings of his cage,
A fever in his topaz eyes;
Disdainful of the rigid bars
His searching cannot pierce between,
Indifferent to his watchers' gaze,
Who note his spotted coat but miss
The fever in his baffled eyes
And anxious twitching of his tail,
He marches back and forth, alone
With his untamed perplexity.

And every hour his moving feet
Pad faster up and down the space
To which impatience limits him,
And as they move, his watchers' eyes
Grow more admiring to observe
The flow of his increasing gait
Along the margin he moves in
And the smooth muscles' play beneath
His rippling skin, and note at length
The fever in his narrowed eyes,
The restless twitching of his tail.

Until, at an expectant time,
When air and sky are still with noon,
He pauses, hearing a bird's voice
From an adjoining prison room,
And the old fever leaves his eyes
Which sought so fruitlessly and long,
And a quick calm enlarges them,
As, though his watchers hardly guess,
A leap of vision shows him how
To trick the challenge of the bars
His busy searchings could not pierce.

And all at once he swings his eyes
From the fixed stripings of the cage
—While the bird sings on, heedlessly—
Toward the bare center of his space,
Then, with a slow, superior grace
Turning his body round one point,
Lolls in the center and is free.

At the Spring

(*Greece*)

The watcher at the spring,
Need he become
Each moving thing he looks upon?
Need he forget, even momently,
The thing he is,
And be the dancing sands he sees
Filter and whirl
Through the rock's thin opening,
Or the turned currents of
Light-catching waters as they pour
Upward and outward, churning through
A gathered water's depth and weight,
Or the half-yielding heads
Of small red water plants
Which ring the pool above
Its bed of gravel-spread limestone?

Why should a watcher so become
Wedded in thought
To any or to all of these
When, if he lies
Still and looks straight down,
With eyes uncaught by any thing
They meet—by dance
Or whirl or leafage or light-play—
Down through to the last sight,
Whichever of them they may see
Will point him always toward the source
From which the waters and
The moving sand
Pour, churn, expand with undeterred
Sheer force, where no man need become
Anything other than he is?

Fathoms

The years of this small white
Fragment of marble that
I plucked from the lost ruin
Of Delphi's god-voiced shrine,
Posed now in a clear space
On my cluttered desk—
The eons it endured
Before the stonecutter
Disjoined it from the stone
Hill's heart that it aged in;
The centuries it passed
Through, while yet in place
Upon the glistening sheer
Pediment or smooth floor;
And the long stretch from when
Some earthquake threw it down
Among the shattered waste
Of that once airy mass,
Till it should catch my eye
During a few hours' stay
Upon the holy hill,
One early spring day: all
Those nameless distances
In time and circumstance
Through which it traveled, from
Its sea bed of soft lime
To this pyramidal
Chance shape it would be called
To take, when finally
It found identity;
All these brief later years
That whirled unseeing past
Its battered uselessness
There in the ageless grass,
While wash of enterprise

Broke upon Greece's shores,
From Rome's despoiling thrusts
To Germany's last rough
Assault, and plain men lived,
Died, struggled, and achieved
Great works and small, as they
Have done perennially—
Now, when I weigh it and
Turn it in my hand
And try to grasp in one
Swelling conception
Years' beyond farther years'
Depending cycles, as
An achieved whole, grow all
But inconceivable.

And since thought behaves quite
The same with each object,
No matter what its size
Or contour, that my gaze
Happens to fall upon
Now while this piece of stone
Dwells in thought's estimate,
I therefore quickly put
It from me and require
This busy mind to ignore
What fathoms of strung years
Compose its universe,
Set the inconspicuous
Rough-cut memento piece
Back in its usual place
On my cluttered desk,
Content that sight should pass
And become as it was
Before my questioning
Caused it and everything
About me to enhance

In depth and reference,
Till they and the whole world
Already seemed dissolved
Into their elements
And the fresh, ripe presence
Of now mouthed and possessed
By a devouring past.

Rhythms

Early or late
Everything falls into place
Everything falls
Under the sun

Time hope fate
Loom and come
Falling lightly each one
On each

And each in turn
Early or late
Lightly falls into place
And falls

And for some other
Makes room
When its small day's
Term is run

As fate comes
Between its hope and time
Calling the day well spent
Or ill

Under the sun
Everything falls into place
Early or late
Everything falls

To See Them

To see them as they are would be
Not to see them,
But to be them:
How then break away
Out of the web that holds you fast
And bids attention only see them?
Break out of the words' net
That will not set you free,
Into the living light
Of living sight?

How but forget
The very meshes of the net:
The words, the phrases, clauses,
Grammar, cadences, and pauses—
Borrowed, begged, or stolen,
Age on age,
Out of a dreaming mind
Too much enamored of its dream?

But how forget? How but distill
Mind and will
Into an emptiness that yet
Is more than all:
That watches and accepts
(But not defines, not glosses,
Not explains)
Each object, each event
In being's complement,
Losses no longer counting losses,
Gains no longer gains?

But to watch them still would be
Only to see them,
Not to be them,

Till the watcher came to see
With something more than a watcher's eye;
Till his seeing learned to pierce
Past his own identity
To creation's nameless core,
Where his seeing self has stood
From before the start of time,
Ageless, dateless,
And aware;
Know the breath that livens him
And the life that breathes in them
Wedded till the end of time
In perpetual interview:

Seeking nothing,
Nothing shunning,
Owning all yet nothing owning,
Taste the saps they're pulsing with;
Past all pretense of believing,
Taking freely,
Freely giving,
Find the substantive of faith
In coevalness with them.

Far is near
And near is far
When you see them as they are.

Edge of Desert

Here at this edge of desert, where
With a half turn
We can arrange to see things bare;
Where the bright, silent sand
Stretches beyond
Assay or comprehension—here
Where wind-stirred, clashing fronds
Of palm and the glow of fruit
Make up what speech
Joins relative to absolute,
Hinting of things
That hover just outside thought's reach
(Here where we stand,
Each one of us, twice every day)—
To say even anything much
Passing the bounds
Of ordinary needs and purposes
Sounds shrill and somehow out of place.

So to acknowledge our blind part
In the illusive play
The shadows of the moving leaves
Elaborate and extend
Toward the bare, glistening sand
Or the green jungle down behind
Only poignantly reminds
Attentive thought
That earthiness is yet
Its very fiber and sap;
That though it may
Look out beyond the distinct edge
Of restless green
To the far sweep of sand and sun,
Yet it must turn, for steadying,

Back to the soil that fostered it,
Telling itself that still
Fruits grow there that refresh and heal.

A Guide

(While Playing a Kyrie of Frescobaldi's)

If, as the old Egyptians held,
Each soul must get him a sure guide
Through the uncertain landscapes of
What countries lie beyond the grave;

And if they took, to serve them there,
Wall-painted lists for counselor,
Which should repeat to the Last Judge
What right deeds sealed their privilege

And steer them, too, up the dim way
That pointed toward their destiny;
And since that seems a sensible
Precaution for a modern soul

Who is no more prepared than those
Egyptians for the way that lies
Before his blindness—I hereby
Take this compelling *Kyrie*

Of Frescobaldi's for my guide
And counsel on death's other side,
Whose flowing periods I play here
Show, painted on the shaken air,

All I, at least, would care to have
Achieved before I cross the grave,
And point, as well, a falterless
Ascent up the dim road to peace.

Fugal Movement

Swing
Swing your fragments round
O Time here as we pass
Brightly swing round
Let fall
Lightly the glancing shards
Fire-spangled as struck glass
Now as we here
In our slow unbelieving
Circle this shrouded stair
On which we slowly move
Through obscure night ascending
To surer realms
And clearer nightless air
And a still ending
Of our poor failing fear
Swing
O swing round your glancing
Lights that as we pass
We may no longer cry
Harshly our unbelief
Into your too attending ear
But fitly hymning your
Cool sure unstaying flow
Toward a new seeing
Coolly surely go
Wrapt in our unresolved
Defeats but knowing now
What thing it is they hide
Within the clouded web
Of fragments you strew round
And thickly now O Time
O swiftly flowing
Thickly then let fall
The strewn shards everywhere

Till always as we move
Along our unclear way
Toward the one ending given
In whose brief seeking
Is our whole hint of heaven
And in whose long avoiding
Our hint of hell
We may be celebrating
Only the nameless light
Darkly held hidden here
Swing
Swing your fragments round
O Time that still we may
And always now be moving
Brightly attended
Lightly turn and pass
In our meek celebrating
And still be gay
Be sad be circling the dim stair
Through night ascending
Out of this heaven and hell
To wider nightless realms
And a still ending
Swing O Time
Swing your strewn fragments round
Here as we pass
This little anxious while
Through our dusk dream
Through clouded webs of seeming
All light within
If only we did know
What spring of unwed light
Attends us where we go
Shining
Quit of all desire
And as we tread
Our timeward circling way

Rays through the dark enclosing air
The quickness of its flame
To catch and gayly gleam
Fire-spangled as struck glass
The falling fragments that you here
Swing round O Time
Swing round us as we pass
In our slow unbelieving
Along this shrouded stair
Toward surer cloudless realms
Where we forever
Were and shall be
And are.